ROYAL WEDDING POEMS

COLLECTED IN ST ANDREWS
TO CELEBRATE THE MARRIAGE OF PRINCE WILLIAM AND MISS KATE MIDDLETON.

(photo be Celeste Slomon)

"Royal Wedding Poems"

Inspiration on the fly
Published by PoemCatcher Creations
Salisbury Centre
2 Salisbury Road
Edinburgh, EH165AB

Cover Design by Trevor at Fresh Digital
ISBN 978-0-9567645-1-5

this book was made over 4 days of poem catching in St Andrew's. It marks the 1st year of poemcatching and the 10th book.

Visit www.poemcatcher.com for other titles.
QUAKE – Built from nothing
BALLS from the queue (Wimbledon tennis)
FUNGUS Poems
SALTY poems from the Sea
FANTASTIC FIREWORKS
HAUNTED HALLOWEEN

About PoemCatcher Creations

The pavement PoemCatcher wanders the streets of festivals and events begging for fresh poems to be written "on the fly". Nearly every poem that is donated gets published, creating books with poetic snapshots that capture the public experience and delight the reader.

He has done this since sitting down on a pavement in march 2010 to beg for poems for the poeple of Haiti.

By spontaneously asking "DONATE A POEM" he inpires brilliance, encourages "raw creativity" and fundraises for charity.

www.poemcatcher.com
inspiration@poemcatcher.com

Dear Prince William and Kate,

Congratulations on your engagement and marriage. Its such an exciting time and I wish you the very best.

The poems you have inspired have been brilliant, creative and very varied. I'm thrilled to have had too many poems for the book, and while it saddens me to leave some out, I have enjoyed the editorial privilege of making a "Royal" collection.

Best wishes on behalf of the authors,

PoemCatcher

Thanks

To Shelagh
For typing the first 30 poems and for feeding me but mostly for sending me the first poems for this book. Your poems inspired me in my own moments of doubt. Without them there may be no book.

To Owen and the staff of Jannetas
For the generous use of the cafe for my fringe show – and the yummiest ice-cream in St Andrews (See my poem Heavenly Hash)

To Radka and housemates at Albany Park
for your hospitality and enthusiastic support

To Matthew and the crew who invited me St. Patricks Day dinner. Yum!

To Onya, on whose computer I made this book.

To the Poets
You amaze me.

Table of Contents

Prologue

Here in our little town their story starts.

Where all our famous ghosts have played their parts.

Two students find their feet and lose their hearts,

Crowning six hundred years of history.

(Dear St. Andrews, 'ever to be the best.')

We wish them joy.

The rest .....

Is mystery.

By Helena Winnicka

WEDDING DRESS

Show us your legs

You met each other on Scottish soil
Now we're having a wedding Royal
Kate will wear a stunning gown
But what about William with his Princes crown.
Hope he doesn't make a choice that's easy
Like something black by Ben De Lisi
Instead make our nation hearten
Why not wear a suit of tartan
or look at the way that you are built
Show us your legs and wear a kilt.

By Shelagh Fraser

Kate's Fate

There once was a girl called Kate
Little did she know her fate
When a see-through dress she dared
and the Prince; he was ford.
She was soon to be more than a mate

By KRWR

A Change of dress

POEM TITLE: _A Change of Dress._

If they have a chance, they
should take it. Young people
in love are always in fashion,
without the weight of oil
portraits in galleries in
palaces staring down, wondering,
like every one else seemingly,
what a royal princess
would wear.

By J Mcteown

13

Wedding Dress Sonnet

Who will make the wedding dress
Galliano, Gaultier, Gucci, Guess,
Missoni, McArtney or Moschino,
Vivienne Westwood or Valentino?
Perhaps she'll wear a Donatella
As she weds her princely fella.
We'll all be looking at the style
As she's escorted up the aisle
Asymetric, floaty or meringue
Or in the style of Vera Wang
Dressed in Primark or in Prada
Arriving in limousine or in Lada
She will be a radiant beauty
As she carries out her royal duty.

By Shelagh Fraser

GIFTS

Wedding gift

The royal wedding will soon be upon us,
I don't understand about all the fuss
I am still waiting for my invite
Maybe then the wedding would bring some delight
I WOULD HAVE BOUGHT THEM A TOASTER!

By Megan Binkley

Gift from the Heart

What do you buy as a gift for the Royal Wedding?
Towels, Le Creuset or some crisp cotton bedding?
No - instead of giving them unwanted dishes
I send them freely all my best wishes
For a life full of fun and love and laughter
And hopes it will be for ever after.

By Shelagh Fraser

HOLIDAY

Good on you

I'm not one of those
Who goes in for the whole
Royal Wedding shannanigans
But you know what?
I really like the idea of a
Free day off...
So good on you
Kate and Wills...

By Nick Anderson

Royal Stag

As William and Kate prepare to marry
My thoughts are turning to best man Harry
What on earth will he plan for the stag
Something outrageous like bagging a WAG?
Or lap dancing club for a bit hokey cokey
Maybe down the local to sing karaoke?
No doubt what it is they'll all land up drunk
As long as Harry lays off the skunk
And forgets about going in fancy dress
Look what happened last time - oh what a mess!
Anyway boys - just go out and play
Don't do anything to threaten our public holiday!

By Shelagh Fraser

A Right Royal Holiday Day

Thank you to the royals,
William and his wife to be.
Hope they have a wonderful wedding day.

An extra days holiday;
means the world to me!
Cheers to the future king and queen.

By Miss Blossom

JEALOUSY OF THE PRINCE HUNTERS

If only.....

If the Prince had come to St Andrews in 2007
He and I would now be in wedding bliss heaven
With banter and chat to rival all others
And frequent tea and cakes with our mothers

The marriage would be cemented on top of a hill
Where the contents of our hearts we would spill
All this said, I think Kate is brill!
And she will be very happy with charming Will.

By Alison Ambrose

You win, Kate

Oh Kate, with your hair so glossy and blown,
From our fine stable of privilege you have flown.
In your engagement photos you looked rather hot,
though while you were here I noticed you not,
In those heady days I spent my time drunk,
Indeed I was lucky not to flunk,
And for this reason (Only) Wills chose not me,
Alas, Why I never a princess shall be.

(It would seem indeed I have little to say,
Perhaps next time I should write a play)

By Holly Patrick

Prince William An Ode

Oh Prince William!
Why didn't you wait.
For us Sallies' girls still waiting at the gate
Alas! It's now too late,
And you shall suffer your fate,
Oh, why Kate, why Kate!
Oh Prince William!

By Sarah Leith

It should have been me

It should have been me –
ring on my finger
and a flash of brown hair,
my arm over his,
but if it were me
I wouldn't have time
to write poetry!

By Isabel Galleymore

We like William and Catherine

Jessica and Helen-
One in a million
Enjoy the glimmering crown
That soon will rest on Will's brow.

I, myself, and not such a fan
Basically I'm jealous
Of that exceedingly lucky man

One day he'll rule
And I'll be just a gangly village fool.

By C P Williamson

The Hunt for the prince

I came from New York
To reclaim the Prince William
I hope to get him

By Rebecca Hunt

Our Prince

We heard people came to St.Andrews
to find their princes,
And we couldn't agree more!

We have found our very own
In a smashing red kilt
Thankyou, poemcatcher
We will be back

xxx Tita & Georgie

Still Hope

Lovely William & Kate
April 29th – that's the date!
When they will marry
But there's still Harry –
So ladies,
There's no need to hate!

By S. Reese

WE LOVE YOU

They met in the name of Charity

POEM TITLE They met in the name of Charity.

She's a beauty, he's a baldy
Watch his hair recede
They've come to save the empire
In its time of need.
His hairline's moving slowly backwards,
Hopefully we're not
They seem a little sketchy
But I guess they're all we've got

By Stephen McKelvie & Kathleen Smith

32

Patrick's Will

POEM TITLE Patrick's Will

Everyone is wearing green.
Prince, will you be King?
Enough smoke; ~~and you~~
you can't see the fire,
Emerald desire.

By Kathleen Smith

Happy Ever After

The bride-to-be knows
What she's letting herself in for,
Has seen what could happen
Headlined in tabloids:
Comparisons with her fiance's mother

She's brave, then,
Marrying her Prince.
I wish them the happy ever after.

By EE Chandler

Cherry stones for Kate

Tinker, Windsor castle
Tailor, Saville Row
Soldier, Head of regiment
Sailor, Heave ho-
Rich man – Very rich man
Poor man – more's the pity
Beggar man, beggars belief
Which of ya will be the thief

Tinker, tailor, soldier, sailor
Every marriage is a failure
Yet marriage is a common fate
These are cherry stones for Kate

By Sally Evans

A lovely little ditty

Will and Kate,
I won't be late,
To attend that wedding date.

It must be fate,
That the future leader
of our sovereign state,
Has finally found
his one true soul mate.

By Andrew and Rachel

Wedding donation

William and Kate are
getting married next month to
each other. Cheers all!

By Kevin Coughlin

Ode to Kate

A Bouncer-Butcher from Blackpool,
Has refound faith in the love pool.
I found a rich man with a £10 bill
His name is the Royal Prince Will.
Soz Kate – better luck still.

By Harriet Fowler

New Beginning

Spring awakening
New love, new life together
A journey begun.

By Anon

California Red Hot Chilli Peppers

Wills and Kate, they are the team
Brought together by a dream

All they do is smile
Will they ever walk a mile

In the shoes they want to claim
Quit playing common games

By Alex B

ST ANDREWS

Auld Grey Toon

St Andrews by the Northern Sea
Home of Golf; University
Cathedral, Castle
working harbour,
train station, all has-beens;
but sixty cafe's, twenty pubs
show what is now the scene
We'll have a day out -
Get in the car
St Andrews isn't very far
But bring a scarf & gloves & brolly
and ask your dad for a bit more lolly

By Judith Harding

St "Match–maker" Andrews

For the love of a woman
Found in a town
Cropped in red wool
Now sharing a gown
The love story made public
The beaches, the wife
The small holes and nine irons
of little town fife

By Jack McGowan

Love in St Andrews

POEM TITLE <u>LOVE IN ST ANDREWS</u>

PERCHED ON THE ROCKY CLIFFS, BY THE
   NORTH SEA,
LIES THE TOWN OF ST. ANDREWS, HAPPY
   AS CAN BE,
STUDENTS COME FROM FAR AND WIDE, ALL
   AROUND THE WORLD,
IN SPORTS, SOCIETIES, PUBS AND THE LIBRARY
   THEIR LOVE WILL BE UNFURLED!
ROMANTIC MOMENTS CAPTURED AGAINST THE RAIN,
SNOW AND COLD,
   LOVE GROWS AND BLOSSOMS IN ST ANDREWS,
   TOGETHER WE'LL GROW OLD.

By Kirstie Macmillan

North Point

POEM TITLE __North Point__

Find us on North Street.
Royaltea served here daily.
((Camera flashes too.)

By Katie Allen

St Andrews poem

POEM TITLE _St Andrews Poem_

It's not haar
here: you can see
he sea.

By Judith Taylor

On the royal wedding

North Point, your one pound coffees
Little did we know
Doormen, Barristers, pre dawn cleaners
Mouthless witnesses, to the monarchical love making-
Kate and Will's met here
(The cheeky parenthesis, for coffee)
But does it matter?
They have their own bop now
And country houses, and Hello magazine,
Great teeth
The whistling clean of fairytale cups

By Barny Quinn

Proposition-Preposition

In St Andrews
by the sea
under pressure
in the lens
under the microscope
in the papers
over the top
in love
on one knee
in the abbey
in the carriage
in the future
on the throne

By Simon Maclaren

Will and Kate

In St Andrews they did meet
So on South, North or Market Street...

Around Kinburn, the quad and Drouthy's did they roam,
And they did share a fight of foam....

Now they're headed for Westminster,
Will Princess Kate end up a spinster?

One thing's for sure, all the world will celebrate,
Apart from the tax payers.... they're irate.....

By Luke Monro

A Royal Meeting

There's not a café in St Andrews
Where will and Kate
Have not met
For the very first time

I wonder what the town means
Small streets, a saintly name
And such an opportunity
To make a future Queen
In the small spaces
Between happy hour, two for one coffees
And a shared sandwich

By Jack McGowan

St Andrews Revisited

A crisp winter morning
In a peaceful seaside town
the cod grabbing tight hold
of all who dare venture outside
And yet the streets are lines with people
all shivering with anticipation
as they wait.

The ancient university town
eager and excited
awaits the return of its two alumni
students in the crowd dream
one day when I return
I too will receive a royal welcome
tutors and professors shaking my hand
- it was a pleasure to teach you
- I remember you well
It seems only fair!

An old woman whispers to her neighbour
- I am a Royalist
and can't wait to shake their hand.
Don't they make a beautiful couple,
I wish them well!

Silence suddenly descends on the crowd
everyone feels the moment has come
People stretch their necks
trying to get a glimpse
as St Andrews is revisited
by Kate and Wills.

By Radka Jersakova

To His Royal Majesty

(Rap and Beatbox Required)

Y'all
I'm heading
To dat royal wedding

I'm gonna steal Kate
As my date
For it is fate

By Sarah and The Easy Street Crew

KISSES
AND MORE...

A Royal Snog

There once was man called Will
Who decided to go in for the kill
Snogged a girl named Kate
Took her out on a date
Now they're engaged, its flipping brill!!!

By Jessica Broomhall and Elin James Jones

The Prince and the Frog

Kate came to St Andrews and found a prince....
I came to St Andrews and found a frog....

Here's Hoping!

By Jennie Lewis

Stiff upper lip

Snogging in public not allowed
Awfully British, far too proud

By Andrew

Oi'll give it a miss

I'd pay cash not to miss
a passionate kiss
But Oi'll be dreading
the Royal Wedding

By Duncan Gillies Maclaurins

"The Kiss"

You say they're sixteen
I say their nineteen
Twenty at a push!

Sitting on a bench
outside Janettas
sharing an ice-cream
with her hand up his sweater.

His lips meet hers
in a mature pucher
and we all wonder
are they lovers...

By Thomas Munro

Lines on the Royal Wedding

Do you take this woman?
Do you take her to have and to hold
but particularly to have, repeatedly,
on the horse-hair stuffing
of the bed of your ancestors
while the footman waits, discreetly,
till you're spent, then steps in
to remove the royal prophylactic?

Do you promise to love this woman,
love and honour her? Not the
constitutional imperatives of love,
but the eyes-rolled-back abandon
of the union, the fizz of lust
that bursts as she divests herself
of ermine-trimmed bikini
and whispers in your ear *Your...Majesty*.

Do you promise to obey?
Obey, *obey* the things which no-one
should ignore – the glory of the orb
and sceptre, weighed in trembling hands,
shyly in the shadowed light, then curious,
then unashamed and commonplace,
a part of what you are, inevitable
as the changing of the guard.

By Andy Jackson

PEOPLE'S PALACE

Marmite

The Royals are like Marmite
Can be a bit sticky
Are re-cycled from living waste
And if you spread them on toast
They are good to taste.

To keep things short
This should be said as it ought,
The Royals are like Marmite
Love them or hate them.

By Colleen

Royal Sock

A lone sock lay
On the bedroom floor
It seemed no other
Lay nearby
Is there another
Such as I?
It seemed to me
I heard it cry
Indeed there were many
Such as she
Some ankle length
Some to the knee
All in need of company
From another such as he?

By Caroline Scott

Face

My hair blows, my heart
pounds,
Your new face is a mystery
Not knowing
Not expecting
Your new face worth the while
Hands touch
My heart pounds

By Anna and Kenzie

One too many beers

Wills and Kate,
Isn't it great
You went on a date.
Met in a town named after a saint
Only a matter of time
Till you consume too much tequila and lime
Wills and Kate, you'll no
longer like this rhyme.

By Anna and Kenzie

Royal Wedding

I don't give a pee
For any jubilee,
Except that it's a woman and a man
who found love for an entire life span.

All the best.
Peace I'm out.

By Martina Jefcoat

Waity Katie

There was a young woman named Kate
Who had such a long time to wait
Then her Prince did propose
The rock on her finger now shows
April 29th will be her wedding date.

By Rachel

Pretention in Irony Minor

Upon this great and happy day, sing of
joy and wond'rous light, O Muse that I've
but small, inferior men, may gaze in some
rhapsodical delight, nay, O'erwhelmed
at such pure tincture, dripp'd from brow so sweet
in waking dream, anticipation sweet.
If only one so small, so pathetic
could glimpse but fleeting glance of this great love
that we, the pleb, have naught bar reflection
then thee, my dear reader, could grasp at truth,
the happiness that natur'ly you are
of course forbid, for you have not the funds!

By Joseph Cunningham

Thanks

If you could greet a Star
A life factory, with the juices of
Love, art, emotions
Brewing in its depths -
If you could gaze into its
All seeing eye
And know the secrets of the universe,
The past and the present blurred
Into a moment of radiant, all -consuming beauty...
What would you say?

By Rachel Bailey

A Royal Limerick

There once was a prince named Will
His life was no terrible thrill
'Till he met a girl named Kate
and took her out on a date
And we hope they live happily ever after...still

By Leslie Jenkins

Royal Occasion

The hands of fate have weaved their loom,
Anticipation to see the groom,
Pass the eye so wee can see
the happy couple of royalty.
On their journey they start today
We wish them happiness
and Joy all the way

By Charlotte Maindron

Violet Melody

Voice that melts
into the cool shapeless form
of night

flash of violet upon my soul

By Suzannah Evans

Crowds

What on earth is this
Parties all over the streets
Someone shouts "I will"

By LM

Woman in the dark

Her eyes grey and sober in the dark

She thinks of angels wings
and other sad beautiful things

In her mind is a pool of water,
And she stirs it slowly

A blue warmth surrounds her

By Suzannah Evans

As a shell of the sea

As a shell comes unexpectedly
From the ocean
As your meeting arrived from the sky
Blessing your souls.
The other half of you is
As the other half of the shell,
Every part needs the other one.
Whenever you forget this,
The voice of the sea
Will bring you here:
Where the boy met the girl and
The girl met the boy
To remember you
That the sky wants you as two parts of the
same shell
Which go back to the ocean
When the waves decide to bring I.

By Stefania

Kate

Kate
===

Burberry queen,
　　Making young girls green,
　She has waited to realise
　　Love's young dream....

By Ruth

Kate and Will

Kate and Will
Jacks and Jill
Fred and Ginger
Perfect together

By Amy Anderson

Princes, Ladies and Thrones

I'll get that lady a throne
Said the Prince
Ladies love thrones
Said the prince
But if the lady is a Prince
Then who gets throne

By Isaac Kim and Tim Han

Coffee Shop Ode

THE ROYAL POEM CATCHER CAUGHT US

AS ITE PASSED US BY

TO SEND A VERSE TO THE ROYAL COUPLE

ALTHOUGH TO ME THIS WAS A

GREAT TROUBLE !

By Big Mac

Epithalamium

POEM TITLE Epithalamium

I asked the Poet
What's all the fuss about
"Will & Kate," he said.
Don't Know 'em, I replied
But I wish them all the best

Bob Holman

By Bob Holman
(USA Slammaster)

Wee country hoose

On her wedding day
Princess Kate will be looking
Like an English rose
Or certainly something floral
After it's over their St Andrews
mates will be looking for an invite
To their wee country hoose in
Balmoral.

By Graeme McGomagal Baxter

The day before the wedding

The sun is lacking
But the ice cream is cracking
The games have been fun
But the day's nearly done
But back home to Dundee
I be packing

By Becca Hunt

Friendship

Never ever try to examine friendships
because friends are like diamonds
When you hit them, they don't break
But may slip away from your life.

By Faisal Fallah

The wedding day

So I wake up in the morning,
With the sun behind a cloud
I go and grab some ice cream
With my American friends who are way too loud
There's a guy in a kilt
Who's quite tall & built
He's super cool, sick and fly,
Glad we met one hell of guy!
But now we must say goodbye
Because to the royal wedding we must fly

By Kali Beach

It began when the joey was born

POEM TITLE It began when the joey was born.

The boxing kangaroo
will deliver the lost shoe
while the princess arrives
in the gold mercedes.

By Sarah McFetridge

Money, churches and polar bears

So I hear you're getting married
Yeah, I guess that's cool
But in a few years, when she takes your money
You will look like a fool
Now I'm not saying she's a gold digga
But I hear she doesn't mess with poor people
Just know that it's more fun to be a lone prince
When you walk into that steeple
O what a right and true travesty
That all the honest girls can confirm
If you ever meet a polar bear
He will crush you like a worm

By Stephen Lavender

Time

Kate, Kate, Kate.
I do believe in fate
Yes since our first date
but please, please, please
when tha big day arrives
don't be <u>late</u>.

By D Bell

Dog Collar

If I were to preside
O'er Wills and Kate
A Royal Wedding be,
I'd read to them
of love, not fate
of joy, where joy can be.

A ministers perspective
can be awful slant
my wish is not directive
but rather just to plant
a seed of the Great Spirit
between the hearts of them
Who chose to wed together
and live until the end.

If I were to preside
O'er Wills and Kate
A Royal Wedding be
I'd read to them
of love, not fate
A life together free.

I'd leave the verses
of the damned
exclude the talk of hell,
I'd focus on the joy of Love
and chime the wedding bell.

If I were to preside
O'er Wills and Kate
A Royal Wedding be
I'd read to them
of love, not fate
Forever may they see

I'd focus on the liturgy
and not her veil or dress.
I'd call the Holy Spirit
to enter in and bless
the sanctity of marriage
The union of hearts
The Royalty aside
and centred from the start

By Andrew Newman

Noisy

Wanderer Wanderer
Where ever ye shall find
The Solace you are seeking
The quiet of the mind
When all around is natter
Of wedding soon to come
The Royal chitter-chatter
Till April's date is done.

By PoemCatcher

Armchair Guest

William and Kate I sit here and wonder
Has "One" at the Palace just made a blunder
And forgotten to send me my invitation
To the biggest wedding of our nation

No I didn't get one of the coveted passes
And won't be there as you raise your glasses
No pate de fois gras to fill my belly
I'll have to make do and watch on the telly

With a beer in my hand, an armchair guest
I'll still raise my glass with the greatest of zest
And I'll make up the words to my very own toast
"I AM NOT THERE COS MINE GOT LOST IN THE POST."

By Shelagh Fraser

Jannettas

What do you do
When half way through
Your 2-scoop ice-cream cone
You realise that you prefer
The scoop that's first tae disappeer
And soon you'll lick it all away
And just be left to your dismay
With the second scoop
"not such a smash"
As your favourite "Heavenly Hash"

By PoemCatcher

*"Heavenly Hash" is my new favourite flavour in my new
favourite ice-cream shop in the whole wide world. Yummy.
(31 South Street, St Andrews)*

Write your poem here...

List of Authors

www.ingramcontent.com/pod-product-compliance
Lightning Source LLC
Chambersburg PA
CBHW072151020426
42334CB00018B/1963